The Everyday Day to Day Weekly

Academic Planner!

@ Journals and Notebooks

Copyright 2016

Reminders:

_____
_____
_____
_____

Monday

Subject	Today's Date: / /	Notes

Tuesday

Subject	Today's Date: / /	Notes

Wednesday

Today's Date: / /

_____
_____
_____
_____

Homework

Homework Due Date: / /

_____
_____
_____

Reminders:

Subject	Today's Date: / /	Notes

Thursday

Subject	Today's Date: / /	Notes

Friday

Saturday

Today's Date: / /

Sunday

Today's Date: / /

Reminders:

Subject	Today's Date: / /	Notes

Monday

Subject	Today's Date: / /	Notes

Tuesday

Wednesday

Today's Date: / /

Homework

Homework Due Date: / /

Reminders:

Subject	Today's Date: / /	Notes

Thursday

Subject	Today's Date: / /	Notes

Friday

Saturday

Today's Date: /   /

Sunday

Today's Date: /   /

Reminders:

Subject	Today's Date: / /	Notes

Monday

Subject	Today's Date: / /	Notes

Tuesday

Wednesday

Today's Date: / /

Homework

Homework Due Date: / /

_____
_____
_____
_____

Thursday

Subject	Today's Date: / /	Notes

Friday

Subject	Today's Date: / /	Notes

Saturday

Today's Date: /   /
_____
_____
_____
_____

Sunday

Today's Date: /   /
_____
_____
_____

Reminders:

Monday

Subject	Today's Date: / /	Notes

Tuesday

Subject	Today's Date: / /	Notes

Wednesday

Today's Date: / /

Homework

Homework Due Date: / /

Thursday

Subject	Today's Date: / /	Notes

Friday

Subject	Today's Date: / /	Notes

Saturday

Today's Date: /   /

Sunday

Today's Date: /   /

Reminders:

Monday

Subject	Today's Date: / /	Notes

Tuesday

Subject	Today's Date: / /	Notes

Wednesday

Today's Date: / /

Homework

Homework Due Date: / /

Reminders:

Subject	Today's Date: / /	Notes

Thursday

Subject	Today's Date: / /	Notes

Friday

Saturday

Today's Date: / /

Sunday

Today's Date: / /

Reminders:

_____
_____
_____

Monday

Subject	Today's Date: / /	Notes

Tuesday

Subject	Today's Date: / /	Notes

Wednesday

Today's Date: /   /

_____
_____
_____
_____

Homework

Homework Due Date: /   /

_____
_____
_____

Reminders:

_____
_____
_____
_____

Subject	Today's Date: / /	Notes

Thursday

Subject	Today's Date: / /	Notes

Friday

Saturday

Today's Date: /   /

_____
_____
_____
_____

Sunday

Today's Date: /   /

_____
_____
_____
_____

Reminders:

Subject	Today's Date: / /	Notes

Monday

Subject	Today's Date: / /	Notes

Tuesday

Today's Date: / /

Wednesday

Homework Due Date: / /

Homework

Reminders:

Subject	Today's Date: / /	Notes

Thursday

Subject	Today's Date: / /	Notes

Friday

Today's Date: /   /

Saturday

Today's Date: /   /

Sunday

Reminders:

_____
_____
_____
_____

Monday

Subject	Today's Date: / /	Notes

Tuesday

Subject	Today's Date: / /	Notes

Wednesday

Today's Date: /   /
_____
_____
_____
_____

Homework

Homework Due Date: /   /
_____
_____
_____

Reminders:

_____
_____
_____
_____

Thursday

Subject	Today's Date: / /	Notes

Friday

Subject	Today's Date: / /	Notes

Saturday

Today's Date: /   /
_____
_____
_____
_____

Sunday

Today's Date: /   /
_____
_____
_____

Reminders:

_____
_____
_____
_____

Monday

Subject	Today's Date: / /	Notes

Tuesday

Subject	Today's Date: / /	Notes

Wednesday

Today's Date: / /

_____
_____
_____
_____

Homework

Homework Due Date: / /

_____
_____
_____

Reminders:

Thursday

Subject	Today's Date: / /	Notes

Friday

Subject	Today's Date: / /	Notes

Saturday

Today's Date: / /

Sunday

Today's Date: / /

Reminders:

_____
_____
_____
_____

Monday

Subject	Today's Date: / /	Notes

Tuesday

Subject	Today's Date: / /	Notes

Wednesday

Today's Date: /   /
_____
_____
_____
_____

Homework

Homework Due Date: /   /
_____
_____
_____

Reminders:

Subject	Today's Date: / /	Notes

Thursday

Subject	Today's Date: / /	Notes

Friday

Saturday

Today's Date: / /

Sunday

Today's Date: / /

Reminders:

Subject	Today's Date: / /	Notes

Monday

Subject	Today's Date: / /	Notes

Tuesday

Wednesday — Today's Date: / /

Homework — Homework Due Date: / /

Reminders:

Subject	Today's Date: / /	Notes

Thursday

Subject	Today's Date: / /	Notes

Friday

Saturday — Today's Date: /   /

Sunday — Today's Date: /   /

Reminders:

_____
_____
_____

Subject	Today's Date: / /	Notes

Monday

Subject	Today's Date: / /	Notes

Tuesday

Wednesday

Today's Date: /   /

_____
_____
_____

Homework

Homework Due Date: /   /

_____
_____

Thursday

Subject	Today's Date: / /	Notes

Friday

Subject	Today's Date: / /	Notes

Saturday

Today's Date: /   /

Sunday

Today's Date: /   /

Reminders:

Subject	Today's Date: / /	Notes

Monday

Subject	Today's Date: / /	Notes

Tuesday

Wednesday Today's Date: / /

Homework Homework Due Date: / /

	Subject	Today's Date: / /	Notes
Thursday			

	Subject	Today's Date: / /	Notes
Friday			

Saturday — Today's Date: / /

Sunday — Today's Date: / /

Reminders:

Subject	Today's Date: / /	Notes

Monday

Subject	Today's Date: / /	Notes

Tuesday

Wednesday

Today's Date: /   /

Homework

Homework Due Date: /   /

Reminders:

Subject	Today's Date: / /	Notes

Thursday

Subject	Today's Date: / /	Notes

Friday

Saturday — Today's Date: / /

Sunday — Today's Date: / /

Reminders:

Subject	Today's Date: / /	Notes

Monday

Subject	Today's Date: / /	Notes

Tuesday

Wednesday

Today's Date: /   /

Homework

Homework Due Date: /   /

Reminders:

Subject	Today's Date: / /	Notes

Thursday

Subject	Today's Date: / /	Notes

Friday

Saturday — Today's Date: / /

Sunday — Today's Date: / /

Reminders:

_____
_____
_____

Subject	Today's Date: / /	Notes

Monday

Subject	Today's Date: / /	Notes

Tuesday

Wednesday

Today's Date: /   /
_____
_____
_____
_____

Homework

Homework Due Date: /   /
_____
_____
_____

Reminders:

Subject	Today's Date: / /	Notes

Thursday

Subject	Today's Date: / /	Notes

Friday

Saturday

Today's Date: / /

Sunday

Today's Date: / /

Reminders:

Subject	Today's Date: / /	Notes
Monday		

Subject	Today's Date: / /	Notes
Tuesday		

Wednesday — Today's Date: /   /

Homework — Homework Due Date: /   /

Reminders:

Subject	Today's Date: / /	Notes

Thursday

Subject	Today's Date: / /	Notes

Friday

Saturday

Today's Date: / /

Sunday

Today's Date: / /

Reminders:

_____
_____
_____
_____

Subject	Today's Date: / /	Notes
		.

Monday

Subject	Today's Date: / /	Notes

Tuesday

Wednesday

Today's Date: / /
_____
_____
_____
_____

Homework

Homework Due Date: / /
_____
_____
_____

Reminders:

Subject	Today's Date: / /	Notes

Thursday

Subject	Today's Date: / /	Notes

Friday

Saturday

Today's Date: / /

Sunday

Today's Date: / /

Reminders:

_____
_____
_____

Monday

Subject	Today's Date: / /	Notes

Tuesday

Subject	Today's Date: / /	Notes

Wednesday

Today's Date: /   /
_____
_____
_____

Homework

Homework Due Date: /   /
_____
_____
_____

Reminders:

_____
_____
_____
_____

Thursday

Subject	Today's Date: / /	Notes

Friday

Subject	Today's Date: / /	Notes

Saturday

Today's Date: /   /

_____
_____
_____
_____

Sunday

Today's Date: /   /

_____
_____
_____

Reminders:

_____
_____
_____
_____

Monday

Subject	Today's Date: / /	Notes

Tuesday

Subject	Today's Date: / /	Notes

Wednesday

Today's Date: /   /
_____
_____
_____
_____

Homework

Homework Due Date: /   /
_____
_____
_____

Reminders:

_____
_____
_____
_____

Thursday

Subject	Today's Date: / /	Notes

Friday

Subject	Today's Date: / /	Notes

Saturday

Today's Date: /   /
_____
_____
_____

Sunday

Today's Date: /   /
_____
_____
_____

Reminders:

_____
_____
_____
_____

Monday

Subject	Today's Date: / /	Notes

Tuesday

Subject	Today's Date: / /	Notes

Wednesday

Today's Date: /   /
_____
_____
_____
_____

Homework

Homework Due Date: /   /
_____
_____
_____

Reminders:

Thursday

Subject	Today's Date: / /	Notes

Friday

Subject	Today's Date: / /	Notes

Saturday

Today's Date: / /

Sunday

Today's Date: / /

Reminders:

Subject	Today's Date: / /	Notes

Monday

Subject	Today's Date: / /	Notes

Tuesday

Wednesday

Today's Date: /   /

Homework

Homework Due Date: /   /

_____
_____
_____
_____

Thursday

Subject	Today's Date: / /	Notes

Friday

Subject	Today's Date: / /	Notes

Saturday

Today's Date: /   /
_____
_____
_____
_____

Sunday

Today's Date: /   /
_____
_____
_____

Reminders:

_____
_____
_____
_____

Monday

Subject	Today's Date: / /	Notes

Tuesday

Subject	Today's Date: / /	Notes

Wednesday

Today's Date: /   /

_____
_____
_____
_____

Homework

Homework Due Date: /   /

_____
_____
_____

Thursday

Subject	Today's Date: / /	Notes

Friday

Subject	Today's Date: / /	Notes

Saturday

Today's Date: / /

Sunday

Today's Date: / /

Reminders:

Subject	Today's Date: / /	Notes
	Monday	

Subject	Today's Date: / /	Notes
	Tuesday	

Wednesday

Today's Date: / /

Homework

Homework Due Date: / /

Reminders:

Subject	Today's Date: / /	Notes

Thursday

Subject	Today's Date: / /	Notes

Friday

Saturday

Today's Date: / /

Sunday

Today's Date: / /

Reminders:

Subject	Today's Date: / /	Notes

Monday

Subject	Today's Date: / /	Notes

Tuesday

Wednesday — Today's Date: / /

Homework — Homework Due Date: / /

Reminders:

Subject	Today's Date: / /	Notes

Thursday

Subject	Today's Date: / /	Notes

Friday

Saturday

Today's Date: /   /

Sunday

Today's Date: /   /

Reminders:

Subject	Today's Date: / /	Notes

Monday

Subject	Today's Date: / /	Notes

Tuesday

Wednesday

Today's Date: / /

Homework

Homework Due Date: / /

Reminders:

_____
_____
_____
_____

Thursday

Subject	Today's Date: / /	Notes

Friday

Subject	Today's Date: / /	Notes

Saturday

Today's Date: /   /
_____
_____
_____
_____

Sunday

Today's Date: /   /
_____
_____
_____

Reminders:

Subject	Today's Date: / /	Notes

Monday

Subject	Today's Date: / /	Notes

Tuesday

Wednesday

Today's Date: /   /

Homework

Homework Due Date: /   /

Reminders:

Subject	Today's Date: / /	Notes

Thursday

Subject	Today's Date: / /	Notes

Friday

Today's Date: / /

Saturday

Today's Date: / /

Sunday

Reminders:

Subject	Today's Date: / /	Notes

Monday

Subject	Today's Date: / /	Notes

Tuesday

Wednesday

Today's Date: / /

Homework

Homework Due Date: / /

Reminders:

_____

_____

_____

_____

Thursday

Subject	Today's Date: / /	Notes

Friday

Subject	Today's Date: / /	Notes

Saturday

Today's Date: / /

_____

_____

_____

_____

Sunday

Today's Date: / /

_____

_____

_____

Reminders:

Subject	Today's Date: / /	Notes

Monday

Subject	Today's Date: / /	Notes

Tuesday

Wednesday — Today's Date: / /

Homework — Homework Due Date: / /

Thursday

Subject	Today's Date: / /	Notes

Friday

Subject	Today's Date: / /	Notes

Saturday

Today's Date: /   /

Sunday

Today's Date: /   /

Reminders:

Subject	Today's Date: / /	Notes

Monday

Subject	Today's Date: / /	Notes

Tuesday

Wednesday

Today's Date: / /

Homework

Homework Due Date: / /

Reminders:

_____
_____
_____
_____

Thursday

Subject	Today's Date: / /	Notes

Friday

Subject	Today's Date: / /	Notes

Saturday

Today's Date: / /
_____
_____
_____
_____

Sunday

Today's Date: / /
_____
_____
_____

Reminders:

Subject	Today's Date: / /	Notes

Monday

Subject	Today's Date: / /	Notes

Tuesday

Wednesday

Today's Date: / /

Homework

Homework Due Date: / /

Reminders:

Subject	Today's Date: / /	Notes

Thursday

Subject	Today's Date: / /	Notes

Friday

Saturday

Today's Date: / /

Sunday

Today's Date: / /

Reminders:

Subject	Today's Date: / /	Notes

Monday

Subject	Today's Date: / /	Notes

Tuesday

Wednesday

Today's Date: / /

Homework

Homework Due Date: / /

Thursday

Subject	Today's Date: / /	Notes

Friday

Subject	Today's Date: / /	Notes

Saturday

Today's Date: / /

Sunday

Today's Date: / /

Reminders:

_____
_____
_____

Subject	Today's Date: / /	Notes

Monday

Subject	Today's Date: / /	Notes

Tuesday

Wednesday

Today's Date: /   /
_____
_____
_____
_____
_____

Homework

Homework Due Date: /   /
_____
_____
_____

Reminders:

Thursday

Subject	Today's Date: / /	Notes

Friday

Subject	Today's Date: / /	Notes

Saturday

Today's Date: / /

Sunday

Today's Date: / /

Reminders:

Subject	Today's Date: / /	Notes

Monday

Subject	Today's Date: / /	Notes

Tuesday

Wednesday

Today's Date: /   /

Homework

Homework Due Date: /   /

Reminders:

Subject	Today's Date: / /	Notes

Thursday

Subject	Today's Date: / /	Notes

Friday

Today's Date: / /

Saturday

Today's Date: / /

Sunday

Reminders:

Subject	Today's Date: / /	Notes

Monday

Subject	Today's Date: / /	Notes

Tuesday

Wednesday

Today's Date: /   /

Homework

Homework Due Date: /   /

Thursday

Subject	Today's Date: / /	Notes

Friday

Subject	Today's Date: / /	Notes

Saturday

Today's Date: / /

Sunday

Today's Date: / /

Reminders:

Subject	Today's Date: / /	Notes
Monday

Subject	Today's Date: / /	Notes
Tuesday

Wednesday

Today's Date: / /

Homework

Homework Due Date: / /

Reminders:

_____

_____

_____

_____

Thursday

Subject	Today's Date: / /	Notes

Friday

Subject	Today's Date: / /	Notes

Saturday

Today's Date: / /

_____

_____

_____

Sunday

Today's Date: / /

_____

_____

_____

Reminders:

Subject	Today's Date: / /	Notes

Monday

Subject	Today's Date: / /	Notes

Tuesday

Wednesday — Today's Date: /   /

Homework — Homework Due Date: /   /

Reminders:

Thursday

Subject	Today's Date: / /	Notes

Friday

Subject	Today's Date: / /	Notes

Saturday

Today's Date: /   /

Sunday

Today's Date: /   /

Reminders:

_____
_____
_____

Subject	Today's Date: / /	Notes

Monday

Subject	Today's Date: / /	Notes

Tuesday

Wednesday

Today's Date: / /
_____
_____
_____
_____

Homework

Homework Due Date: / /
_____
_____
_____

Reminders:

_____

_____

_____

_____

Thursday

Subject	Today's Date: / /	Notes

Friday

Subject	Today's Date: / /	Notes

Saturday

Today's Date: /   /

_____

_____

_____

_____

Sunday

Today's Date: /   /

_____

_____

_____

Reminders:

Subject	Today's Date: / /	Notes

Monday

Subject	Today's Date: / /	Notes

Tuesday

Wednesday

Today's Date: /   /

Homework

Homework Due Date: /   /

Reminders:

Thursday

Subject	Today's Date: / /	Notes

Friday

Subject	Today's Date: / /	Notes

Saturday

Today's Date: / /

Sunday

Today's Date: / /

Reminders:

Subject	Today's Date: / /	Notes

Monday

Subject	Today's Date: / /	Notes

Tuesday

Wednesday

Today's Date: / /

Homework

Homework Due Date: / /

Thursday

Subject	Today's Date: / /	Notes

Friday

Subject	Today's Date: / /	Notes

Saturday

Today's Date: /   /

Sunday

Today's Date: /   /

Reminders:

_____
_____
_____
_____

Monday

Subject	Today's Date: / /	Notes

Tuesday

Subject	Today's Date: / /	Notes

Wednesday

Today's Date: /   /
_____
_____
_____
_____

Homework

Homework Due Date: /   /
_____
_____
_____

Reminders:

Subject	Today's Date: / /	Notes

Thursday

Subject	Today's Date: / /	Notes

Friday

Saturday

Today's Date: / /

Sunday

Today's Date: / /

Reminders:

Subject	Today's Date: / /	Notes
Monday		

Subject	Today's Date: / /	Notes
Tuesday		

Wednesday — Today's Date: / /

Homework — Homework Due Date: / /

Reminders:

Subject	Today's Date: / /	Notes

Thursday

Subject	Today's Date: / /	Notes

Friday

Saturday

Today's Date: /   /

Sunday

Today's Date: /   /

Reminders:

Subject	Today's Date: / /	Notes

Monday

Subject	Today's Date: / /	Notes

Tuesday

Wednesday

Today's Date: /   /

Homework

Homework Due Date: /   /

Reminders:

Subject	Today's Date: / /	Notes

Thursday

Subject	Today's Date: / /	Notes

Friday

Saturday

Today's Date: / /

Sunday

Today's Date: / /

Reminders:

Subject	Today's Date: / /	Notes

Monday

Subject	Today's Date: / /	Notes

Tuesday

Wednesday

Today's Date: / /

Homework

Homework Due Date: / /

Reminders:

_____
_____
_____
_____

Thursday

Subject	Today's Date: / /	Notes

Friday

Subject	Today's Date: / /	Notes

Saturday

Today's Date: /   /
_____
_____
_____
_____

Sunday

Today's Date: /   /
_____
_____
_____

Reminders:

Subject	Today's Date: / /	Notes

Monday

Subject	Today's Date: / /	Notes

Tuesday

Wednesday — Today's Date: / /

Homework — Homework Due Date: / /

Reminders:

Thursday

Subject	Today's Date: / /	Notes

Friday

Subject	Today's Date: / /	Notes

Saturday

Today's Date: /   /

Sunday

Today's Date: /   /

Reminders:

_____

_____

_____

	Subject	Today's Date: / /	Notes
Monday			

	Subject	Today's Date: / /	Notes
Tuesday			

Wednesday — Today's Date: /   /

_____

_____

_____

Homework — Homework Due Date: /   /

_____

_____

_____

Reminders:

Subject	Today's Date: / /	Notes

Thursday

Subject	Today's Date: / /	Notes

Friday

Saturday

Today's Date: / /

Sunday

Today's Date: / /

Reminders:

_____

_____

_____

Monday

Subject	Today's Date: / /	Notes

Tuesday

Subject	Today's Date: / /	Notes

Wednesday

Today's Date: / /

_____

_____

_____

Homework

Homework Due Date: / /

_____

_____

_____

Thursday

Subject	Today's Date: / /	Notes

Friday

Subject	Today's Date: / /	Notes

Saturday

Today's Date: /   /

Sunday

Today's Date: /   /

Reminders:

Subject	Today's Date: / /	Notes

Monday

Subject	Today's Date: / /	Notes

Tuesday

Wednesday

Today's Date: / /

Homework

Homework Due Date: / /

Thursday

Subject	Today's Date: / /	Notes

Friday

Subject	Today's Date: / /	Notes

Saturday

Today's Date: /   /

Sunday

Today's Date: /   /

Reminders:

Subject	Today's Date: / /	Notes

Monday

Subject	Today's Date: / /	Notes

Tuesday

Wednesday

Today's Date: / /

Homework

Homework Due Date: / /

Reminders:

_____
_____
_____
_____

Thursday

Subject	Today's Date: / /	Notes

Friday

Subject	Today's Date: / /	Notes

Saturday

Today's Date: / /

_____
_____
_____
_____

Sunday

Today's Date: / /

_____
_____
_____

Reminders:

_____
_____
_____
_____

Subject	Today's Date: / /	Notes

Monday

Subject	Today's Date: / /	Notes

Tuesday

Wednesday

Today's Date: / /
_____
_____
_____
_____

Homework

Homework Due Date: / /
_____
_____
_____

Reminders:

_____
_____
_____
_____

Thursday

Subject	Today's Date: / /	Notes

Friday

Subject	Today's Date: / /	Notes

Saturday

Today's Date: /   /
_____
_____
_____
_____

Sunday

Today's Date: /   /
_____
_____
_____

Reminders:

Subject	Today's Date: / /	Notes

Monday

Subject	Today's Date: / /	Notes

Tuesday

Wednesday

Today's Date: /   /

Homework

Homework Due Date: /   /

Reminders:

_____
_____
_____
_____

Thursday

Subject	Today's Date: / /	Notes

Friday

Subject	Today's Date: / /	Notes

Saturday

Today's Date: /   /

_____
_____
_____
_____

Sunday

Today's Date: /   /

_____
_____
_____

Reminders:

Subject	Today's Date: / /	Notes

Monday

Subject	Today's Date: / /	Notes

Tuesday

Wednesday

Today's Date: / /

Homework

Homework Due Date: / /

Reminders:

Subject	Today's Date: / /	Notes

Thursday

Subject	Today's Date: / /	Notes

Friday

Saturday

Today's Date: /   /

Sunday

Today's Date: /   /